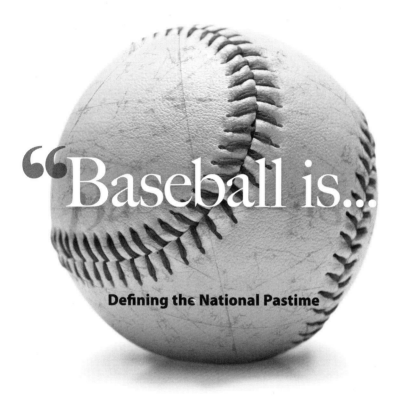

"Baseball is...

Defining the National Pastime

EDITED BY PAUL DICKSON

Dover Publications, Inc. | Mineola, New York

Copyright

Copyright © 2011 by Paul Dickson
All rights reserved.

Bibliographical Note

Baseball Is: Defining the National Pastime is a new work, first published by Dover Publications, Inc., in 2011.

Library of Congress Cataloging-in-Publication Data

Baseball is— : defining the national pastime / [compiled by] Paul Dickson.
  p. cm.
Includes bibliographical references.
ISBN-13: 978-0-486-48209-5
ISBN-10: 0-486-48209-X
1. Baseball—Quotations, maxims, etc. I. Dickson, Paul.
GV867.3.B338 2011
796.357—dc22
                                        2010048397

Manufactured in the United States by Courier Corporation
48209X01
www.doverpublications.com

BOOK AND COVER DESIGN BY PETER DONAHUE

THE MULTI-DEFINITIVE BOOK ON THE NATIONAL PASTIME

The first rule in baseball's rule book, 1.01, starts with these two words "Baseball is..." and goes on to say "a game between two teams of nine players each, under direction of a manager, played on an enclosed field in accordance with these rules, under jurisdiction of one or more umpires."

As a lifelong fan and sometimes writer on the subject of baseball, I have been long fascinated with the two words "Baseball is..." Over the course of the last decade or so, I have collected hundreds of definitional lines, and what is amazing is how many ways the definition can be finished.

What follows are some of the most amusing, diverse, and informative ends to the subject and verb. A few explanatory notes are in order first. If a name appears in quotation marks, that means that the quotation was made by a fictional character. There are a small handful of quotations which do not actually contain the exact two words; they are rare and are only included because it would have been a misdemeanor not to include them. So, there are a few *has been*'s, *was*'s, *is not/isn't*'s, and one or two *is baseball*'s.

In addition, while in the process of collecting these from friends and acquaintances who framed responses for the compendium, some of these worked and others didn't. I have included several of these and indicated they were from friends rather than collected from traditional sources.

"Baseball is...

Defining the National Pastime

EDWARD ABBEY

"Baseball is a slow, sluggish game, with frequent and trivial interruptions, offering the spectator many opportunities to reflect at leisure upon the situation on the field: This is what a fan loves most about the game."

—American writer (1927–1989).

RHONDA ABRAMS

"Baseball is a sport of statistics. On Opening Day, every team's record is perfect. The whole season is ahead of them."

—From her business column in USA Today, *April 9, 2010*

GEORGE "SPARKY" ANDERSON

"Baseball is a simple game. If you have good players, and if you keep them in the right frame of mind, then the manager is a success. The players make the manager; it's never the other way."

—*The former player as Cincinnati Reds manager. Anderson, who also managed at Detroit, once said: "A baseball manager is a necessary evil."*

ROGER ANGELL

"Baseball is mostly low-lights, but baseball movies must suggest otherwise, often by edited, close-up snatches of bats meeting balls, gloves gobbling up grounders, spiked feet toeing a base, and so on."

—"The Sporting Science," The New Yorker, *July 31, 1989.*

"Baseball is simple but never easy."

—Widely attributed, perhaps his most famous line.

ANONYMOUS

"Baseball is an island of activity amidst a sea of statistics."

"In the great department store of life, baseball is the toy department."

ATLANTA BRAVES' WIVES

"Baseball is … packing alone, driving 1,500 miles across the country alone with three children (all under six) to join your husband's new team."

"Baseball is … buying your World Series wardrobe a week before the season ends—only to be beaten out in the last game of the year by the Dodgers."

"Baseball is … watching your husband sing Happy Birthday to Charlie Finley's mule."

Charlie Finley and the A's mascot, Charlie O., the Missouri mule.

"Baseball is ... hearing the man behind you call your husband a bum."

"Baseball is ... the weeks and months following your husband's injury, wondering if he'll be able to play again."

—From a much longer list of "Baseball is..." one-liners composed by this group of player's wives and quoted in The Sporting News, *August 7, 1971.*

EVE BABITZ

"Baseball is easy to fathom, not like football, which people explain to me at great length and I understand for one brief moment before it all falls apart in my brain and looks like an ominous calculus problem. The tension in baseball comes in spurts between long waits where everyone can forget about it, a perfectly lifelike rhythm."

—The American writer from "Dodger Stadium," from Slow Days, Fast Company, *first published in* Cosmopolitan, *1974.*

RUSSELL BAKER

"Baseball is the slowest sport this side of long-distance needlepoint."

—Columnist, New York Times, *March 6, 1993.*

RED BARBER

"Baseball is my favorite sport ... because it is orderly. Football is organized confusion. Even the coaches don't know anything about it until they get it on film. And basketball is just fellows running up and down in their under shorts."

–*Quoted in* Red Barber, *by Barbara Grizzuti Harrison, c. 1991.*

MIKE BARNICLE

"Baseball is our best game. It teaches kids patience as well as perseverance. It teaches them how to win and how to lose."

—*From his* Boston Globe *column, May 6, 1998.*

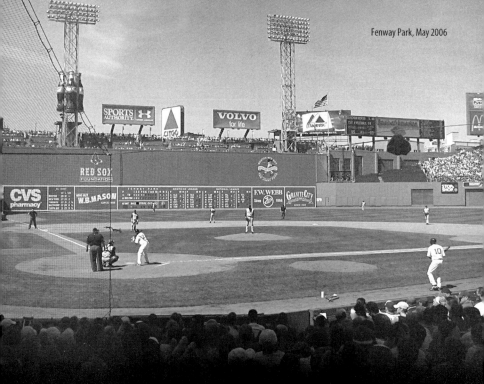
Fenway Park, May 2006

ALLAN BARRA

"Baseball is the only major sport in which stadiums matter."

JACQUES BARZUN

"Baseball is a kind of collective chess with arms and legs under full play under sunlight."

—God's Country and Mine: A Declaration of Love Spiced with a Few Harsh Wards. *Boston: Little, Brown and Co., 1954.*

"Baseball is Greek in being national, heroic, and broken up in the rivalries of city-states. How sad that Europe knows nothing like it. Its Olympics generate anger, not unity, and its interstate politics follow no rules that a people can grasp. At least Americans understand baseball, the true realm of clear ideas."

That baseball fitly expresses the powers of the nation's mind and body is a merit separate from the glory of being the most active, agile, varied, articulate, and brainy of all group games. It is of and for our century.…The idea of baseball is a team, an outfit, a section, a gang, a union, a cell, a commando squad—in short, a twentieth-century setup of opposite numbers."

—God's Country and Mine: A Declaration of Love Spiced with a Few Harsh Wards. *Boston: Little, Brown and Co., 1954.*

BASEBALL ALMANAC

"Baseball is the only professional sport where every single thing that every player on the field does is recorded— good or bad. Mark McGwire even once commented that during his seventy home run season the media was counting the number of cups of coffee he actually drank each and every day."

> —*From the Introduction to its online section on statistics,* http://www.baseball-almanac.com.

11

GERALD BEAUMONT

"Baseball is a peculiar profession, possibly the only one which capitalized a boyhood pleasure, unfits the athlete for any other career, keeps him young in mind and spirit, and then rejects him as too old before he has yet attained the prime of life."

—*From* Hearts and the Diamond, *Dodd, Mead and Company, 1921.*

New York Giants, 1905.

MARK BELTAIRE

"Baseball is almost the only place in life where a sacrifice is really appreciated."

—*As a sportswriter for the* Detroit News.

IRA BERKOW

"Baseball is a pleasant pastime, a genial undertaking, a civil essay. Football is war. Baseball is a kid's game. You put on a beanie and knickers to play it. In football, you don armor."

—*"For Jackson, What Choice?"* The New York Times, *June 24, 1986. (Sports of the Times). The Jackson in question was Bo Jackson, who was deciding which sport to play professionally.*

YOGI BERRA

"Baseball is ninety percent mental. The other half is physical."

—One of the most often stated "Berraisms;" Berra has stood by this one. "It may be 95 percent or it may be only 80, but anybody who plays golf, tennis, or any other sport knows what I mean," is how he put it in his autobiographical work, Yogi: It Ain't Over.

"Little League baseball is a very good thing because it keeps the parents off the streets."

—From Yogi: It Ain't Over.

"Baseball is the champ of them all. Like somebody said, the pay is good and the hours are short."

—Quoted in The Sporting News, *November 21, 1951.*

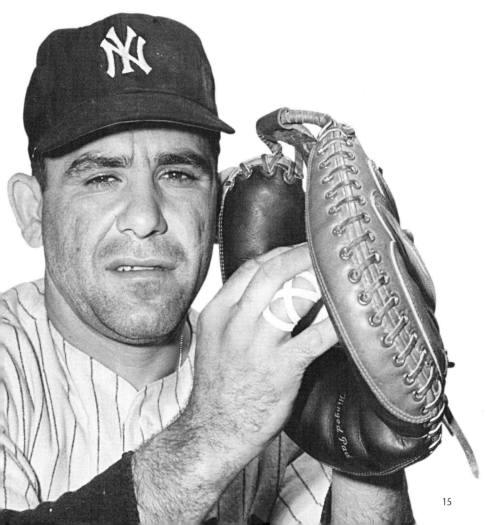

15

HARRY BLACKMUN

"Professional baseball is a business and it is engaged in interstate commerce—and thus normally subject to federal business law. But it is in a very distinct sense an exception and an anomaly. The aberration is an established one."

—The Supreme Court justice delivering the 5-3 majority opinion that upheld the owners in a suit brought by St. Louis Cardinal outfielder Curt Flood vs. Major League baseball, in 1972, upholding baseball's reserve clause.

Curt Flood

HAL BODLEY

"Baseball is America's pastime, the summertime game that allows us to slip back to our childhood and break away from the stresses of daily life. There's no escaping what happened to us Tuesday. Hoping Bonds blasts home run No. 64 against Houston, or the Rocket improving his record to 20-1 or teams in crucial games trying to win playoff berths means absolutely nothing … The heart and soul of our country was torn apart Tuesday, and for now baseball is insignificant."

—*The veteran sportswriter's column in* USA Today, *the day following the 9/11/2001 attacks on America.*

WADE BOGGS

"Baseball is the only sport where you can do everything 100 percent right and still fail."

—Early in the 1993 season when he was making good contact but still hitting into trouble.

THOMAS BOSWELL

"Baseball is not necessarily an obsessive-compulsive disorder, like washing your hands 100 times a day, but it's beginning to seem that way. We're reaching the point where you can be a truly dedicated, state-of-the-art fan or you can have a life. Take your pick.

These days, long-time baseball lovers face tough questions. 'Do you have to be in a Rotisserie league? Is it mandatory to read the Elias Baseball Analyst cover to cover with a highlight pen? If you haven't digested Bill James's latest 598-pager, are you still allowed to express an opinion while in the park?'"

—The Washington Post, *April 13, 1990.*

"Baseball is really two sports—the Summer Game and the Autumn Game. One is the leisurely pastime of our national mythology. The other is not so gentle."

—In How Life Imitates the World Series, *by Boswell, 1982.*

"Baseball is religion without the mischief."

—*Widely attributed.*

THOMAS BOSWELL (CONTINUED)

"Baseball is still the greatest soap opera in sports. That's what keeps reviving the game. It has the most detail, the most vivid characters and, even in the offseason, the most continuous action. Counting spring training and the postseason, baseball can grab your attention more than 250 days a year."

—The Washington Post, *December 16, 1997.*

"Baseball is the home run. It's other stuff, too. But nothing is as central as the homer. The long ball is the focal point of the game, its most important tactical weapon, its most profitable selling point and its central symbol."

—The Washington Post, *April 1, 1996.*

"BASEBALL IS..."

BASEBALL IS.   23

JIM BOUTON

"Baseball is unique among team sports in its glorification of the individual, his opportunity to excel being limited only by his willingness to cooperate in a lawfully delineated competition."

—The Atlantic Monthly, *April 1964.*

"To the fierce, ardent leather-lunged professional fan, baseball is life itself, a motive for breathing, the yeast that helps his spirit, as well as his gorge, rise."

—In *"The Fantasy World of Baseball."*

ERIK BRADY

"Baseball is no longer the nation's most popular sport, as it was during the World War II era, but it is still the sport most connected to our past. And the feeling in the air Monday seemed connected to our past, too—to a time when Ted Williams played for Uncle Sam rather than the Boston Red Sox."

—USA Today *writer on September 18, 2001, Monday, when baseball returned after a self-imposed six days of darkness following the attacks of 9/11.*

Ted Williams serving in the Korean War, 1952.

JIMMY BRESLIN

"Baseball isn't statistics, it's Joe DiMaggio rounding second base."

—*Quoted by Herb Caen in the* San Francisco Chronicle, *June 3, 1975.*

DAVE BRISTOL

"...baseball is a game where you gotta have fun. You do that by winning."

> —*Former manager of the Cincinnati Reds, Milwaukee Brewers, Atlanta Braves, and San Francisco Giants.*

RUPERT BROOKE

"...baseball is a good game to watch, and in outline easy to understand, as it is merely glorified rounders."

> —*The British poet describing baseball as played at Harvard College in 1913; writing in* Letters from America, *1916.*

"DAGWOOD BUMSTEAD"

"Baseball, my son, is the cornerstone of civilization."

—Uttered by the comic strip character in the decades-long running Blondie *comic strip by Dean Young.*

"Baseball is a mirror in which we can see the whole of America—political, social, racial, everything—and its story is an odyssey that helps tell us who we are, because how we play is also who we are."

—The film documentarian who chronicled baseball's history in a nine-part PBS series; quoted in Smithsonian *magazine, July 1994.*

Briggs Stadium, 1942.

"...baseball is life, but life is profits."

— *Filmmaker quoted in an Associated Press piece of June 4, 1999.*

STEVE BUSBY

"Baseball, to me, is still the national pastime because it is a summer game. I feel that almost all Americans are summer people, that summer is what they think of when they think of their childhood. I think it stirs up an incredible emotion within people."

—Pitcher who played his entire career for the Kansas City Royals (1972–76, 1978–80). He batted and threw right-handed. Quoted in The Washington Post, *July 8, 1974.*

34

GEORGE W. BUSH

"Baseball is the style of a Willie Mays or the determination of a Hank Aaron or the endurance of a Mickey Mantle, the discipline of a Carl Yastrzemski, the drive of Eddie Mathews, the reliability of a (Al) Kaline, the grace of a Joe DiMaggio, the kindness of a Harmon Killebrew, and the class of Stan Musial, the courage of a Jackie Robinson, or the heroism of Lou Gehrig."

—At an event at the White House to promote T-ball during which Hank Aaron, Yogi Berra, Ernie Banks, and other Hall of Famers lunched at the White House with the country's baseball fan-in-chief. Milwaukee Journal Sentinel, *March 31, 2001.*

VANNEVAR BUSH

"Baseball is like air travel; things move fast for a small part of the time. But they do not move so fast that the fans cannot follow them. And the fans participate vicariously in the strategy involved, more so than in any other sport. This is what keeps them coming and paying for tickets. It is why they learn, and keep up to date on, reams of statistics, many of them faulty or misleading. It is why they are relatively uninterested in any sport of analysis other than their own.

"It is a grand game, even if it could be a lot better, even if its use of statistics is foggy and its management occasionally dumb, even if the sports writers and the broadcasters tell us little about it that they have not repeated a thousand times. It is still a grand game because it exemplifies strategy in the raw, and because it has about it an air of mystery."

—*The prominent scientist in "When Bat Meets Ball." In* Science is Not Enough, *New York: William Morrow & Co., 1967.*

JIMMY CANNON

"Baseball is menaced because our institutions are no longer venerated because of their age. The kids believe baseball is hokey because the game's spokesmen speak pompous nonsense. The financiers should shut up and let the players act out the pantomime of their game in decent silence. The crack of the bat striking the ball in modern baseball is drowned out by the noises of the owners yelling about money."

—*Sportswriter, 1969. From* "Nobody Asked Me, But …" *1978.*

JIM CAPLE

"A lot of people say that baseball is no longer our national pastime. And they're right. That's because the new national pastime is bashing baseball."

—Commentator on ESPN, Page 2. September 10, 2010. He explained: "At least, that's the media's favorite pastime outside of telling us such important news as which celebrities are cheating on their spouses. No matter what happens, the media trashes baseball, while lavishing a man-crush of praise on the NFL. No matter the facts, the storyline is always that baseball is as hopelessly irrelevant and stubbornly out-of-date as dial-up connections, VHS tapes and intelligent political debate. Critics throw so many beanballs and cheap shots at baseball that you practically need to don batting helmets and protective cups just to listen to talk radio or read a column."

GEORGE CARLIN

"Baseball is played on a diamond, in a park. … Football is played on a gridiron, in a stadium. Baseball begins in the spring, the season of new life. Football begins in the fall, when everything's dying. … In football the object is for the quarterback, also known as the field general, to be on target with his aerial assault. … In baseball the object is to go home! And to be safe! I hope I'll be safe at home!"

—From one of the comedian's most famous routines quoted in his USA Today *obituary, June 24, 2008.*

"Baseball is the only major sport that appears backwards in a mirror."

—Brain Droppings, *1997.*

CLAY CARROLL

"[Baseball is] a hitter's game. They have pitchers because somebody has to go out there and throw the ball up to the plate."

—*As Reds pitcher, widely quoted.*

BRUCE CATTON

"In its essentials, then, baseball is plebeian, down-to-earth, and robustious … There has never been any social cachet attached to skill on the diamond. The reason, obviously, is that baseball came up from the sand lots—the small town, the city slum, and the like. It had a rowdy air because rowdies played it. One of the stock tableaux in American sports history is the aggrieved baseball player jawing with the umpire. In all our games, this tableau is unique; it belongs to baseball, from the earliest days it has been an integral part of the game, and even in the carefully policed major leagues today it remains unchanged, baseball never developed any of the social niceties."

—*The Civil War historian writing "The Great American Game,"* American Heritage, *April 1959.*

FRANK CERESI

"Baseball is neatly defined kinetic energy."

—*Attorney and baseball collector extraordinaire.*

TWO MEN DOWN

HENRY CHADWICK

"Baseball is a recreation that anyone may be proud to excel in as in order to do so, he must possess the characteristics of true manhood to a considerable degree."

—*Baseball pioneer from* Beadle's Dime Base-Ball Player, *New York, 1860.*

THE CHICAGO AMERICAN

"Baseball is one of the reasons why American soldiers are the best in the world … capable of going into action without officers."

—*1906 newspaper editorial. Quoted in George F. Will's* Men at Work, *1990.*

TOM CLANCY

"Baseball is probably the most tactically intricate of team sports because it depends upon a vast set of interlocking variables. Baseball may also be the last place where we can find real sportsmanship: The other team can make a good play, win the game and still the fans will show some appreciation. And without the people who show that appreciation, the people who buy the tickets and eat the hot dogs, the people who bring their sons to demonstrate how the game is really supposed to be played—without them, the owners and players are nothing."

—*The novelist writing as part owner of the Baltimore Orioles in* The New York Times, *March 21, 1995.*

ELLIS CLARY

"Baseball isn't keeping up with science. Satellites are sending accurate signals from outer space to earth, but coaches still have trouble transmitting signals from third base to home."

—*As former Washington Senators third-base coach,* Baseball Digest, *February 1961.*

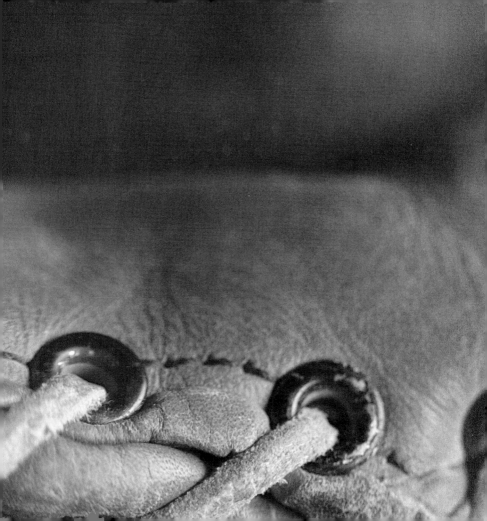

TY COBB

"Baseball is a red-blooded sport for red-blooded men. It's no pink tea, and mollycoddles had better stay out. It's a contest and everything that implies, a struggle for supremacy, a survival of the fittest. Every man in the game, from the minors on up, is not only fighting against the other side, but he's trying to hold onto his own job against those on his own bench who'd love to take it away. Why deny this? Why minimize it? Why not boldly admit it?"

—*Ty Cobb with Al Stump in* My Life in Baseball: The True Record, *Garden City, N.Y.: Doubleday Co., 1961.*

"Baseball is the greatest game in the world."

—*Ty Cobb with Al Stump in* My Life in Baseball: The True Record, *Garden City, N.Y.: Doubleday Co., 1961.*

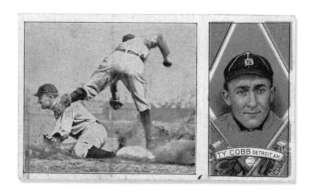

"Baseball is the National Sport and a nation of baseball players never will decay. If it is true that the Battle of Waterloo was won on the cricket fields of Eton, is no less true, perhaps, that America's reputation as a nation sportsman was built on the foundation of baseball fields."

—From the introduction to The Big Baseball Book For Boys By Him.
G. Bonner, 1931.

"I have observed that baseball is not unlike war, and when you get right down to it, we batters are the heavy artillery."

—The 12-time batting crown winner, widely quoted.

MARVIN COHEN

"Baseball is purer than life; it's symmetrical, fair, and dignified. There's no debating what happened: it happened.

"It happened: concretely, empirically. So much so, that the intangibles, the spirit, are the presiding halos over baseball. Records make for legends. Baseball is our great national myth. The crowd roars in unison, or those of it that have in common the art of being the same team's rotting fans. They all pull together. Enthusiasm, hysteria: a common love. Baseball is bigger than us all."

—Baseball the Beautiful: Decoding the Diamond. *New York: Links Books, 1974.*

CHARLES M. CONLON

"The game which seems to breathe the restless spirit of American life, that calls for quick action and quicker thinking, that seems characteristic of a great nation itself, is baseball."

—The great early photographer of baseball portraits from "The Base Ball Photographer," The Photographic Times, *1913.*

COOK COUNTY (ILL.) GRAND JURY

"The jury is impressed with the fact that baseball is an index to our national genius and character … Baseball is more than a national game; it is an American institution, having its place, prominently and significantly in the life of the people."

> —*From final report to Chief Justice Charles A. McDonald regarding the conspiracy by Chicago White Sox players to throw the 1919 World Series, Nov. 6, 1920.*

WHITE SOX 1919

"CHICK" GANDIL
First Base

RAY SCHALK
Catcher

EDDIE CICOTTE
Pitcher

JOE JACKSON

HARRY LIEBOLD

"SWEDE" RISBERG

JOE JENKINS

BILL JAMES

BYRD LYNN

OSCAR FELSCH

EDDIE COLLINS

"BUCK" WEAVER

JOHN COLLINS

DICK KERR

URBAN FABER

CLAUDE WILLIAMS

EDDIE MURPHY

FRED McMULLIN

MICHELE WALTERS COSTA

"To me baseball is a romance, marked by good days and bad, heartaches and thrills, ups and downs, but always with each day promising something new…"

—*Writing in* The Washington Post, *August 1, 1994.*

BOB COSTAS

"Football is weekly, an event. Baseball is daily, a fact of life. Basketball is a greyhound you thrill to. Baseball is a cocker spaniel who steals your heart."

> —*Quoted by Curt Smith in "The Old Ballgame: Baseball Is Increasingly a Thing of the Past. What Happened to the National Pastime?" In the* National Review, *April 1998.*

STANLEY COVELESKI

"Lord, baseball is a worrying thing."

—From "Diamond Quotes" in Nine, *2004 edition. This common quotation has been extracted from a longer one which appeared in George F. Will's* Men at Work, *1990. "The pressure never lets up. Don't matter what you did yesterday. That's history. It's tomorrow that counts. So you worry all the time. It never ends. Lord, baseball is a worrying thing."*

NEWTON CRANE

"Baseball, although the American national game, is not only of English origin, but is one of the most ancient of English sports. In a letter of the celebrated Mary Lepel, Lady Hervey, written in 1748, the family of Frederick, Prince of Wales, are described as "diverting themselves with baseball, a play all who are or have been schoolboys are well acquainted with." It is hardly likely that the modern game of baseball has anything in common with the sport thus referred to. The latter was probably what our grandfathers called "bases," and which, by an easy process of development, became rounders, a sport still indulged in by the youth of both sexes in the North and Midlands, the baseball of the last century was one of the numerous games of ball which, descended from the remotest antiquity, furnish a common origin to cricket and football, as well as to baseball. Of these cricket is perhaps the most scientific, but its claims in that respect find a jealous rival in baseball, which has now reached such a state of perfection, in both batting and fielding, as to leave but little apparent room for further development."

As President of the National Baseball League of Great Britain and former United States Consul, Manchester, from his book Baseball, *published by George Bell & Sons, London, 1891.*

ALVIN DARK

"There are surprisingly few real students of the game in baseball; partly because everybody, my eighty-three-year-old grandmother included, thinks they learned all there was to know about it at puberty. Baseball is very beguiling that way."

—Rookie of the Year in 1948. Dark went on to play fourteen years for six different teams and later to manage five major league teams.

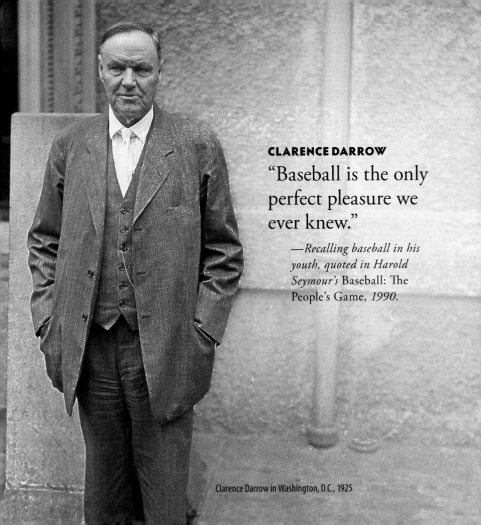

CLARENCE DARROW

"Baseball is the only perfect pleasure we ever knew."

—*Recalling baseball in his youth, quoted in Harold Seymour's* Baseball: The People's Game, *1990.*

Clarence Darrow in Washington, D.C., 1925

Leo Durocher managing the Brooklyn Dodgers, 1939.

LARAINE DAY

"Baseball is a serious thing in this country, and if that reveals our immaturity, I suppose there is little we can do about it until we grow up."

—*The actress wife of Leo Durocher from her book,* A Day With the Giants.

FRANK DEFORD

"Baseball is … all about lineups, and should the new commissioner [A. Bartlett Giamatti] issue any such papal bull as he did during his tenure at Yale, it ought to be in the form of a lineup card, to be posted in hearts and dugouts everywhere. It should read:

HOME TEAM

Green, CF

History, IB

Park, RF

Civility, 3E

Individual, 2B

Croup, SS

Law, LF

Offense, C

Defense, P

There would be no designated hitter."

—*The sports commentator from "A Gentleman and a Scholar."* Sports Illustrated, *April 17, 1989*.

"Baseball is like the train going by in the night and the whistle blowing, and the little boy is lying in bed and he thinks of how the train is going to all sorts of wonderful, mysterious places in the world. And you would see the standings, every day, and they would read: New York, Detroit, Boston, Cleveland, Philadelphia, Chicago, Washington, St. Louis, and it was the most evocative train schedule ever printed."

—*"Coming to Baseball...but Not Necessarily Being Loved Back." In Fimrite, Ron, ed.,* Birth of a Fan, *New York: Macmillan, 1993.*

LARRY DOUGHTY

"Baseball is supposed to be a non-contact sport, but our hitters seem to be taking that literally."

—*As Pittsburgh Pirates general manager, 1989.*

"JIMMY DUGAN"

"Baseball is what gets inside you. It's what lights you up."

—*The Tom Hanks role in the 1992 film,* A League of Their Own, *written by Lowell Ganz and Babaloo Mandel.*

BAIN NEWS SERVICE

"BASEBALL IS…

CHARLES EBBETS

"Baseball is still in its infancy."

—In a speech that he gave before the first game of the 1912 season. In 1960, on the occasion of the cornerstone from Ebbets Field being moved to Cooperstown, an article in the New York Herald Tribune *noted, "Even Ebbets had no idea of how right he was. It was years before the advent of radio, television, night baseball, air transportation, rabbit ball, player representation, pension plan, all-star games, minimum salaries, the negro in baseball and two-platoons." Ebbets's line was one of eight "Famous Baseball Sayings" collected by Ernest J. Lanigan of the Hall of Fame when he identified himself as "Historian and authority on the game for 65 years."*

THOMAS EDISON

"Baseball is the greatest of American games. Some say football, but it is my firm belief, and it shall always be, that baseball has no superior … I have not attended very many big games, but I don't believe you can find a more ardent follower of baseball than myself, as a day seldom passes when I do not read the sporting pages of the newspaper. In this way I keep a close tab on the two major leagues and there was one time when I could name the players of every club in both leagues."

—The St. Petersburg Times, *February 25, 1927, quoted when he was at his Fort Myers, Florida, laboratory.*

ROY EISENHARDT

"Baseball is a terrific radio sport...because radio feeds our imagination. I was a Tiger fan all the time I was growing up, and I have a perfect memory of George Kell and Hoot Evers making certain plays that I heard but never saw. I remember them to this day. I'd be lying out on the gross at home listening to the game, but I was really there in the ballpark. I think baseball has survived all this time because of its place in our imagination—because we've chosen to make the players and the gamer, something larger than they really are. But television has just the opposite of feet. The players are shown so closely and under such a bright light that we lose all illusion."

—*Former Oakland A's president quoted by Roger Angell, "Being Green,"* The New Yorker, *August 15, 1983.*

Briggs Stadium,
Detroit 1946

CHARLES WILLIAM ELIOT

"I think baseball is a wretched game; but as an object of ambition for youth to go to college for, really it is a little weak. There are only nine men who can play the game, and there are nine hundred and fifty men in college; and out of those nine there are only two desirable positions, I understand—pitcher and catcher—so there is but little chance for the youth to gratify his ambition. I call it one of the worst games, although I know it is called the American national game."

—*Harvard University president,* St. Louis Globe-Democrat, *April 12, 1884.*

LACY ELLERBY

"Baseball is business now. I'm glad I played baseball when it was baseball. We had fun."

—Veteran of the Negro baseball leagues who played for four teams between 1937–1954. Quoted in The Washington Post, *November 1, 1997.*

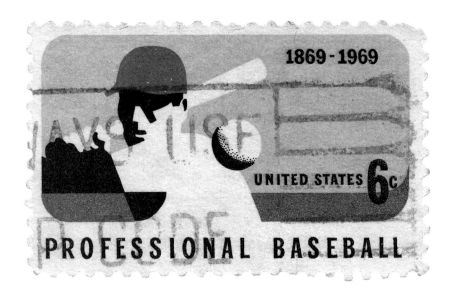

ERIC ENDERS

"Baseball is virtually the only aspect of U.S. culture embraced by the Cuban Revolution, an enterprise based largely on resisting American imperialism."

—From "Through the Looking Glass: The Forgotten World of Cuban Baseball." Nine, *2003.*

JAMES T. FARRELL

"…we like baseball. We like the atmosphere of a ball park, the practice sessions, the warming up of the pitchers, the moment when the home team runs out onto the field for the first inning, the sound of the crack of the bat, the alternating moments of rest and action, the ball arching out to a fielder, or else lifting, rising and disappearing from sight as it goes out of the park, the thrill when a catcher receives a fast ball—briefly, we like baseball. And without rationalizing or devising arguments, we think that perhaps our national life might have been the poorer without it. No other sport is quite the same to many of us. Baseball is a lot of fun."

—The Chicago writer from My Baseball Diary, *New York: A. S. Barnes & Co., 1937. Farrell was an avid baseball fan and well versed in the statistics of the game.*

THAT ARM
YOUR COUNTRY
NEEDS IT

FEATHER RIVER BULLETIN

"Baseball is more than a National Game. It is America's anchor. It keeps the ship of state fast to its moorings in a balanced life. American boys are not conscripted into army service, they play baseball, and "Play ball" is their battle cry, not "Heil Hitler." While little Fascists are learning how to toss hand grenades, little Americans are learning to groove one over the plate. But woe betide the enemy when an American boy finds it needful to throw hand grenades!"

—Feather River Bulletin, *Plumas County, Quincy, Calif., 1939; quoted in Crepeau, Richard C.,* Baseball: America's Diamond Mind, *Orlando: University Presses of Florida, 1980.*

BOB FELLER

"Every day is a new opportunity. You can build on yesterday's success or put its failures behind and start over again. That's the way life is, with a new game every day, and that's the way baseball is."

—*The Hall of Fame pitcher.*

STEVE FIFFER

"One reason baseball is so enduring is because it is both a simple and a complex game."

—How to Watch Baseball, *1987.*

MARC FISHER

"On the radio of the American night, baseball is the security blanket. The clichés lull and comfort as they drift over the AM dial, assuring us that despite these cool spring evenings, summer is truly near. Inside to him. High and tight. Steps off the mound. Setting the defense now … The voices are familiar, fading in and out from Detroit and New York, from Cincinnati and Boston, a pace boys learn from under the pillow after bedtime, the cadence of the American Century."

—The Washington Post *columnist, May 17, 1997. Fisher has written extensively on radio.*

"BASEBALL IS…

GEORGE FITCH

"Baseball is played by a grandstand full of maniacs assisted by eighteen players in uniform, a national commission, a box full of sporting writers, a book of rules as thick as the Illinois code, and a low-browed pirate called an umpire. The object of baseball is to win the game for the home team. To do this it is sometimes necessary for the spectators to yell continuously for three hours at a time. This develops marvelous endurance. There are prominent business men in the United States who can pick out a player 100 yards away during a riot and can address a remark to him which he will not only hear but which will make him fighting mad."

—*Humorous essayist from his "Sizing Up Uncle Sam," 1914.*

F. SCOTT FITZGERALD

"Ring moved in the company of a few dozen illiterates playing a boy's game. A boy's game with no more possibilities than a boy could master, a game bounded by walls which kept out danger, change or adventure."

—On the death of Ring Lardner on September 25, 1933, commenting on what Fitzgerald saw as his unfulfilled promise. From The Crack-Up, *edited by Edmund Wilson, 1945. This quotation and the one on the next page have given rise to a number of hybrid anti-baseball quotations attributed to Fitzgerald along the lines of "baseball is a child's game played by a few dozen illiterates."*

"Baseball is a game played by idiots for morons."

—*Quoted by Raymond Mungo* in Confessions from Left Field, *1983.*

JOE FLAHERTY

"Baseball is the most democratic of games. Unlike football and basketball (and, in reverse snobbery, even the art of being a jockey), size has little to do with achievement and excellence."

—*The journalist from the introduction to Joel Oppenheimer's* The Wrong Season, *1973.*

ELIZABETH BALES FRANK

"Baseball is as sexy as a spectator sport gets…when I say sexy, I mean the nature of the intimacy between the game and its fans, between those who make baseball and those for whom baseball is made, which is all of us. Look at it this way: Football is a game, basketball is a sport, but baseball is a state of mind."

—*Novelist from her essay on baseball and sex which originally appeared in* Cosmopolitan *magazine.*

FREUDIAN INTERPRETATION

"The pitcher-father tries to complete a throw into the mitt of his mate crouched over home plate. A series of sons step up and each in turn tries to intercept the throw. If any of them is successful, he can win "home" and defeat the pitcher—if he is able first to complete a hazardous journey out of the adult world of the father's allies."

—*Thomas Gould,* The Ancient Quarrel Between Poetry and Philosophy, *quoted in New York Times Magazine, September 11, 1983.*

FORD FRICK

"Baseball is a public trust, not merely a money-making industry."

—*Baseball commissioner.*

Baseball Commissioner Ford Frick (left) and National League President William Harridge, July 9, 1937.

FRANK FRISCH

"Baseball is like this. Have one good year and you can fool them for five more, because for five more years they expect you to have another good one."

—*Quoted in* Baseball Wit and Wisdom *by Frank Graham and Dick Hyman, 1962.*

ROBERT FROST

"... some baseball is the fate of all. For my part I am never more at home in America than at a baseball game ... in beautiful weather ... and my side winning."

—*"A Perfect Day—A Day of Prowess,"* Sports Illustrated, *July 23, 1956.*

MONIKA SKOLE FUCHS

"Baseball is something that you don't automatically understand when you are sworn in as an American citizen."

> —*A friend who celebrated her citizenship by attending a Red-Sox-Tampa Bay game at Fenway Park.*

HUGH S. FULLERTON

"[Baseball] is the greatest single force working for Americanization. No other game appeals so much to the foreign-born youngsters and nothing, not even the schools, teaches the American spirit so quickly, or inculcates the idea of sportsmanship or fair play as thoroughly."

> —*Sportswriter, quoted in Riess, Steven A.,* Touching Base: Professional Baseball and American Culture in the Progressive Era. *Westport, Conn.: Greenwood Press, 1980.*

PETER GAMMONS

"Baseball is the best sport to cover because it's *daily*. It's ongoing. You have to fill the need, write the daily soap opera."

—*As a sportswriter for the* Boston Globe. *Hall of Fame Collection.*

JOE GARAGIOLA

"Baseball is a funny game."

> *—The title of his 1960 memoir, which was rebutted in Rogers Hornsby's 1962 memoir* My War with Baseball, *in which he wrote "Joe Garagiola, an ex-ball player, made some money by writing a book called* Baseball Is a Funny Game. *I congratulate Joe on the success of his book, but baseball is not, in my opinion, a funny game."*

"Baseball is a game of race, creed, and color. The race is to first base. The creed is the rules of the game. The color? Well, the home team wears white uniforms, and the visiting team wears gray."

> *—From his 1960 memoir.*

"Baseball is drama with
an endless run and an
ever-changing cast."

—*From his 1960 memoir.*

LOU GEHRIG

"There is no room in baseball for discrimination. It is our national pastime and a game for all."

—The baseball immortal's response to segregated baseball; widely attributed.

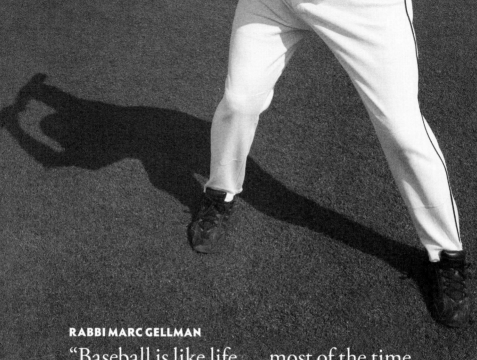

RABBI MARC GELLMAN

"Baseball is like life … most of the time
nothing much seems to happen."

—*Quoted in US News, 1997; from Gellman's appearance on
"Good Morning America."*

A. BARTLETT GIAMATTI

"Baseball has the largest library of law and love and custom and ritual, and therefore, in a nation that fundamentally believes it is a nation under law, well, baseball is America's most privileged version of the level field."

> —*The late Commissioner from "Conversation,"* Sports Illustrated, *April 17, 1989.*

"[Baseball] is designed to break your heart. The game begins in the spring, when everything else begins again, and it blossoms in the summer, filling the afternoons and evenings, and then as soon as the chill rains come, it stops and leaves you to face the fall alone."

> —*"The Green Fields of the Mind,"* Yale Alumni Magazine, *November 1997.*

RICHARD GILMAN

"Baseball is a game dominated by vital ghosts; it's a fraternity, like no other we have of the active and the no longer so, the living and the dead."

The noted critic quoted in Jonathan Fraser Light's The Cultural Encyclopedia of Baseball, *1997.*

PETER GOLENBOCK

"Baseball is a religion. The playing field is sacred, the rules fair and just, and wherever a game is being played, the Gods are smiling."

—Noted baseball historian in a quotation created for this book, September 2010.

"Baseball, like religion, politics, and sex, is an enduring institution that has provided American society with a special, unique outlet for its passions. For many of us the eternal question 'Is baseball a sport or a business?' is irrelevant. Whatever label one attaches to it, what it inevitably becomes is a mania, an obsession, a joyful spending of hours, days, lives devoted to watching, second-guessing, discussing, arguing, analyzing favorite teams, players, games, strategies, moments."

—From the Preface to The Best of Spitball, the Literary Baseball Magazine, *Pocket Books, 1988.*

STEPHEN J. GOULD

"… baseball is profound all by itself and needs no excuses; people who don't know this are not fans and are therefore unreachable anyway."

—The late anthropologist writing in the November 1989 issue of Natural History. *The comment was made in reaction to writers who suggested linkages between the game and "deep issues of morality, parenthood, history, lost innocence, gentleness and so on." This is an effort he says "reeks of silliness." Gould adds that when anyone asks him how baseball imitates life, he responds with a "barnyard epithet."*

RED GRANGE

"Football is work. Baseball is fun."

—*Football great nicknamed "The Galloping Ghost."*

VANALYNE GREEN

"Modern baseball is a game of constantly shifting roles and signifiers, a delicate balance between randomness and order. It is a stage onto which we project our most primitive feelings about the seemingly random events that determine human fate."

—*"Mother Baseball," in: Nauen, Elinor, ed.,* Diamonds Are a Girl's Best Friend: Women Writers on Baseball, *1994.*

ERIC ROLFE GREENBERG

"… baseball isn't anything like life … In truth, nothing in the game appealed to me as much as its unreality. Baseball is all clean lines and clear decisions. Wouldn't life be far easier if it consisted of a series of definitive calls: safe or out, fair or foul, strike or ball. Oh, for a life like that, where every day produces a clear winner and an equally clear loser, and back to it the next day with the slate wiped clean and the teams starting out equal. Yes, a line score is a very stark statement, isn't it? The numbers tell the essential story. All the rest is mere detail."

—*Spoken by the fictionalized character of Christy Mathewson.* The Celebrant, *Lincoln, Neb.: Univ. of Nebraska Press, 1983.*

Christy Mathewson, 1912

Knott Wright by A. C. Hutchison

BARBARA GREGORICH

"Baseball is for the youth in all of us, for those who won't quit, who won't compromise, who would rather go down swinging than give up and play softball."

—*Thoughts of her fictional character Linda Sunshine in her baseball novel* She's on First, *New York: PaperJacks, 1987, 1988.*

DICK GREGORY

"Baseball is very big with my people. It figures. It's the only time we can get to shake a bat at a white man without starting a riot."

—*The African-American comedian from his memoir,* From the Back of the Bus, *1962.*

GEORGE GRELLA

"It requires no giant leap of logic or intuition to recognize that the magical qualities of primitive religion also exist in baseball. The sport is the nearest thing to a national Rite of Spring that all Americans can celebrate and enjoy; no other activity in our country is so closely linked to ritual and myth…Baseball is obviously life-centered and lifegiving, a game of youth and its attendant virtues—grace, growth, joy, and love."

—*"Baseball and the American Dream,"* The Massachusetts Review, *Summer 1975.*

RICHARD GROSSINGER

"Baseball is truly an obscurity. Beside it, dreams and ethnoastronomy are explicit and open books."

—*In the preface to the baseball issue of* IO Magazine.

BRYANT GUMBEL

"…the other sports are just sports. Baseball is a love."

—*As a sportscaster, 1981.*

DONALD HALL

"…baseball is continuous, like nothing else among American things, an endless game of repeated summers, joining the long generations of all the fathers and all the sons."

—The poet from "Fathers Playing Catch With Sons," Playboy, *April 1974.*

"Baseball is fathers and sons. Football is brothers beating each other up in the backyard."

—From "Fathers Playing Catch With Sons," Playboy, *April 1974.*

PETE HAMILL

"Baseball is the sport of a democracy, where the only requirement is talent. You don't have to be a giant to play it. You don't have to be able to fight on ice skates. You don't have to be a 240-pound side of beef, synchronized into a war machine."

—From his essay "Winding up for Spring," The Washington Post, *March 9, 1981.*

KEN "THE HAWK" HARRELSON

"Baseball is the only sport I know that when you're on offense, the other team controls the ball."

—*The All-Star first baseman and outfielder in* Sports Illustrated, *September 6, 1976.*

ERNIE HARWELL

"Baseball is a ballet without music. Drama without words. A carnival without kewpie dolls."

> —*The late, great sportscaster from his famous and oft-quoted 1955 Opening Day* Sporting News *essay "The Game for All America."*

"Baseball is cigar smoke, hot-roasted peanuts, *Ladies' Day*, 'down in front,' … the seventh inning stretch, and the 'Star-Spangled Banner.'"

> —*From his* Sporting News *essay "The Game for All America."*

Broadcaster Ernie Harwell, 1942.

"Baseball is continuity. Pitch to pitch. Inning to inning.
Game to game. Series to series. Season to season."

—*From his* Sporting News *essay* "The Game for All America.

STANLEY HAUERWAS

"… baseball, like life itself, has been and continues to be distorted by sin. I have lost my innocence….Baseball is part of our fallen world. Indeed, it seems that baseball, like the Congress of the United States, is the mirror into which we must look if we are to see ourselves—a sobering thought."

—*Duke University theologian Stanley Hauerwas (in the foreword to:* The Faith of 50 Million: Baseball, Religion, and American Culture, *edited by Christopher H. Evans and William R. Herzog, II, Westminster John Knox, 2002).*

ELROD HENDRICKS

"Baseball is unlike other games in the subtleties it has."

—*The longtime Orioles bullpen coach; quoted in* The Baltimore Sun, *October 10, 2000.*

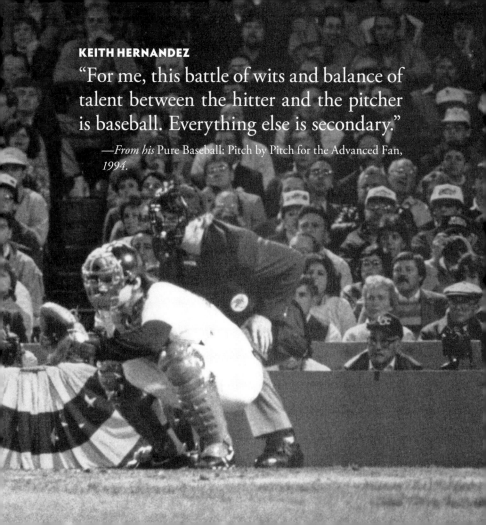

KEITH HERNANDEZ

"For me, this battle of wits and balance of talent between the hitter and the pitcher is baseball. Everything else is secondary."

—*From his* Pure Baseball: Pitch by Pitch for the Advanced Fan, *1994.*

PHIL HERSH

"Baseball is the only game you can see on the radio."

—*The quote appears in nine-inch-high letters in the broadcast exhibit at the National Baseball Hall of Fame and Museum. From "Baseball is a Dream That Can't go Away,"* The Chicago Tribune, *August 11, 1985.*

GEORGE V. HIGGINS

"Baseball is the cruelest sport. Almost every other occupation permits the mediocre performers to seek out his plane of maximum competence, however low, and then lumber along until he reaches retirement age. Baseball ruthlessly eliminates every single young recruit who that year lacks the talent to join that .0000024 percent of the total population of the United States that plays major league baseball (we will leave Latin America and Canada out of the calculation; to include them would only serve to make the statistics more depressing.)"

—*The late novelist from* The Progress of the Seasons, *1989.*

"Baseball, like sex and religion, is a complicated game to play, but not hard to understand."

—*Quoted in Steve Fiffer's* How to Watch Baseball, *1987.*

ART HILL

"It may be that baseball is, under close analysis, pointless. What seems apparent to me is that close analysis is pointless. The game is there. It is the best game there is. That's all you need to know."

—*Sportswriter from* I Don't Care If I Ever Come Back: A Baseball Fan and His Game, *1980.*

CALVIN HILL

"Baseball is sitting on the front porch, drinking lemonade, listening to your father talk to his father or his brothers about the game and things that happened that day. Part of the appeal of baseball now is that it's a reminder of the ways things used to be before we became so transient, so mobile, so much in a hurry. Baseball is stopping by the fence to visit; football is honking the horn.

"Before batting practice, baseball players are kidding around, maybe talking to the fans, while in a football locker room it's like getting ready to jump out of an airplane, or going into battle. Everybody's in his own world, trying to blot out what's about to happen. Baseball players are intense at getting themselves ready, but by comparison with football players they're a bunch of guys getting ready to go fishing or hunting."

—Former professional football player, and vice president for personnel of the Baltimore Orioles. "The Joys of Summer," in Mullarkey, Karen, ed. dir., Baseball in America, *San Francisco: Collins Publishers, 1991.*

WOODY HOCHSWENDER

"The world of baseball is designed to exist outside of fashion and its restless trendiness. In some respects, its very unfashionableness constitutes its allure. 'Almost Chanel, But 100% Polyester.'"

—*Writer in* The New York Times, *July 9, 1991.*

JOHN B. HOLWAY

"Baseball is, after all, a simple game. All it takes to win is to cross home plate more often than the other team."

—*Esteemed baseball historian from his book* Blackball Stars: Negro League Players, *1988.*

HERBERT HOOVER

"The rigid voluntary rules of right and wrong, as applied in American sports, are second only to religion in strengthening the morals of the American people … and baseball is the greatest of all team sports."

—Quoted by Branch Rickey in The American Diamond: A Documentary of the Game of Baseball, *1965.*

—

Herbert Hoover, May 13, 1922

ROGERS HORNSBY

"Baseball is my life, the only thing I know and can talk about. It's my only interest….I'm not a good mixer. I get bored at parties and I bore other people. I don't like to get dressed up and go out."

—*Quoted in Robert Lipsyte's column,* The New York Times, *June 16, 1969.*

FRANK HOWARD

"The trouble with baseball is by the time you learn how to play it, you can't play it anymore."

—Former major league outfielder, 1976.

EDWIN HOWSAM

"Baseball is an ethereal game whose music is orchestrated by a moving sphere."

—Baseball Graffiti, *self-published, 1995.*

KIN HUBBARD

"Knowin' all about baseball is just about as profitable as bein' a good whittler."

—Journalist and humorist Abe Martin's The Best of Kin Hubbard, *edited by David S. Hawes, 1989.*

JEFF IDELSON

"Baseball is a timeless representation of American culture, values and history."

—President, National Baseball Hall of Fame and Museum, Cooperstown, N.Y.

BILL JAMES

"Baseball is a wonderful form of education. The ways we have of learning about baseball are better than our ways of learning about anything else. A young child can acquire knowledge about baseball from television, radio, newspapers, books. The game is open to you if you're a poet or an accountant, if you're a left-brain or a right-brain person. Nothing else in this country does so good a job of teaching the public about itself, I go to games, I listen to games on the radio, I watch some on TV, I check the box scores every morning. I have fantasy teams, I read books. The game is everywhere. Following another sport like that is possible, but it's a lot of work. That's one reason people are into baseball. But the green grass and the blue skies are wonderful, too. An athlete can love basketball as much as he loves baseball—but can a poet?"

— *"Phantoms of the Ballyard," in Karen Mullarkey's* Baseball in America, *San Francisco: Collins Publishers, 1991.*

"Baseball, I think, is essentially a riddle beyond solution."

—*From a Harold Seymour Lecture quoted by Tim Wiles.*

BAN JOHNSON

"Baseball is the sinew and gut of the American spirit."

—American League President who, among other things, was a staunch defender of baseball's exemption from antitrust legislation. When a Congressman questioned the exemption he furiously replied: "That man represents something alien to the American character."

WALTER JOHNSON

"Baseball is simply a dramatization of the life struggle of a man."

—*The Hall of Fame pitcher, quoted by Chester Crowell in the* American Magazine, *1925.*

ROGER KAHN

"Baseball is for the leisurely afternoons of summer and for the unchanging dreams."

—From "Intellectuals and Ballplayers," The American Scholar, *November 3, 1957.*

ROD KANEHL

"Baseball is a lot like life. The line drives are caught, the squibbers go for base hits. It's an unfair game."

—The New York Mets infielder in 1963. Quoted in The Jocks *by Leonard Shecter, 1969.*

JESSE KATZ

" ... baseball is ... a reservoir of oiled mitts and cut grass and fathers and twilight, the attic of American boyhood. It is about the senses, the whispers of memory, that make us care even when the sport falls short of its promise."

—"Artless Dodgers," Los Angeles Magazine, *April 2002.*

"BASEBALL IS...

GARRISON KEILLOR

"Baseball is a game but it's more than a game. Baseball is people, dammit, and if you are around people, you can't help but get involved in their lives and care about them. And then you don't know how to talk to them or tell them how much you care and how come we know so much about pitching and we don't know squat about how to communicate? I guess that is the question."

—*Writer/Performer "What Did We Do Wrong," 1985.*

"Baseball is classic American. Every time you go to the game, you pay homage to your old man. He who lobbed the tennis ball so it bounced off your bat and gave you the thrill of success, who engaged in the patient, silent, intimate conversation playing catch.

"None of us is born smart; each of us needed basic tutoring from Dad. Shoe tying, nail pounding, hoeing, parallel parking and baseball. And now, years later, you sit and watch the game by heart and see the third baseman's heroic backhand stab of the sizzling grounder down the line and his long throw to catch the runner at first, and (involuntarily) you raise a fist and yell, 'Yes!'—it all goes back to your old man."

—*"Divided by politics, united by baseball,"* The Baltimore Sun, *August 17, 2006.*

JIM KERN

"Baseball is much easier if everyone thinks you're an off-the-wall babbling idiot."

—*Texas Rangers pitcher, 1980.*

139

LARRY KING

"But baseball on the radio, as seen through the eyes of those men who made a profession of bringing the game into the mind's eye, is wonderful. When we love our hometown announcer, we love him. We don't like it if somebody else takes over for him for an inning or two. If you're a Dodger fan, you want to hear Vin Scully, just as the Dodger fans of my youth wanted Red Barber and no one else."

—*Television talk show host, from his baseball memoir,* Why I Love Baseball, 2004.

HENRY KISSINGER

"Baseball is the most intellectual game because most of the action goes on in your head."

—*Widely attributed.*

FREDERICK C. KLEIN

"Baseball is the day-in, day-out game of spring, summer and fall, and its threads become part of the fabric of many lives. Somebody wrote that people go to Cooperstown expecting to learn about baseball's past, but discover their own there as well. I've visited the place as man and boy, and can vouch for that."

—*From his* Wall Street Journal *column, December 20, 1996.*

Johnny Podres/Roy Campanella statues commemorating the 7th game of the 1955 World Series, Cooperstown, N.Y.

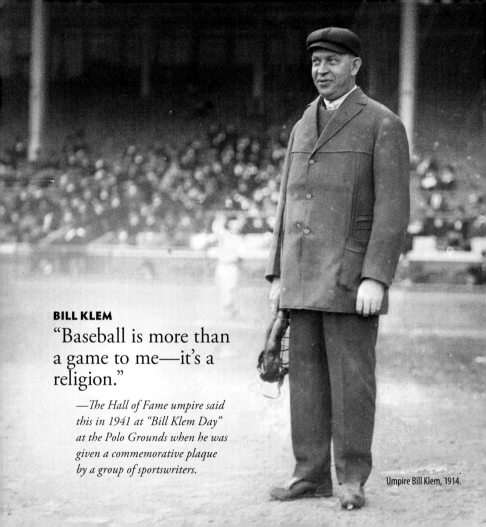

BILL KLEM

"Baseball is more than a game to me—it's a religion."

—*The Hall of Fame umpire said this in 1941 at "Bill Klem Day" at the Polo Grounds when he was given a commemorative plaque by a group of sportswriters.*

Umpire Bill Klem, 1914.

CHARLES KRAUTHAMMER

"Baseball is so modestly republican. The World Series is a continuation of the season by other means. Played in real towns, it is awarded, democratically, to the city with the most wins, not the best caterers. And the players are built to human, yeoman scale. Footballers wear uniforms designed to make them mammoth and interchangeable, like the products of an oversized assembly line. Baseball outfits are meant to betray the real body underneath. In baseball's perfectly American balance of anarchy and order, uniforms are worn. But republican flannels, for God's sake, not the pads and helmets of a Nixonian Swiss guard."

—*The conservative columnist,* The Washington Post, *January 25, 1985.*

BOWIE KUHN

"Baseball is beautiful ... the supreme performing art. It combines in perfect harmony the magnificent features of ballet, drama, art, and ingenuity."

—*As Baseball Commissioner, 1976.*

"EBBY CALVIN 'NUKE' LALOOSH."

"A good friend of mine used to say, 'This is a very simple game. You throw the ball, you catch the ball, you hit the ball. Sometimes you win, sometimes you lose, sometimes it rains.' Think about that for a while."

—*The Tim Robbins character quoting the Kevin Costner character, Crash Davis, in the movie* Bull Durham *(1988). The script was written by Ron Shelton.*

ANNE LAMOTT

"Baseball is so egalitarian—anyone, even a five-foot-two-inch pencil-necked geek can grow up to be a baseball great."

—*"The Psychic Hat," in* Birth of a Fan, *ed. Ron Fimrite, 1993.*

JUDGE KENESAW MOUNTAIN LANDIS

"Baseball is something more than a game to an American boy; it is his training field for life work. Destroy his faith in it squareness and honesty and you have destroyed something more; you have planted suspicion of all things in his heart."

—*As Commissioner of Baseball.*

TOMMY LASORDA

"Baseball is like driving, it's the one who gets home safely that counts."

—*Former player and long-time Dodgers manager.*

BILL "SPACEMAN" LEE

"Baseball is the belly-button of our society. Straighten our baseball, and you straighten out the rest of the world."

> *—From a February 3, 1977,* Los Angeles Times *interview. Lee advocated the return of real grass and nickel beer nights.*

BOB LEMON

"Baseball is a kid's game that grownups only tend to screw up."

> *—As New York Yankees manager, 1979.*

MICHAEL LEWIS

"Baseball is this intense subculture that actually doesn't speak very much for the larger culture."

> —Moneyball, *2003.*

PHIL LINZ

"Baseball is a fun game. It beats working for a living."

—*Infielder for Yankees, Phillies, and Mets.*

ROBERT LIPSYTE

"Baseball is us and we are baseball for better and for worse."

—The New York Times.

MIKE LITTWIN

"Baseball is memory. Baseball is history without wars and famines. It's tragedy without tears. It's Casey at the Bat. It's Mudville."

—*From his* Baltimore Sun *column, March 28, 1986.*

J. ANTHONY LUKAS

" … baseball is a linear game, falling naturally, play by play, inning by inning into a story, an epic tale waiting to be told by men and boys in schoolyards or locker rooms, or late at night around beer-heavy tables."

—The New York Times.

CONNIE MACK

"Baseball is so American.
There is not a hamlet or
village where you will not
find a baseball diamond and
a makeshift team of sorts."

—Connie Mack's Baseball
Book, *1955.*

"BARNEY MANN"

"Baseball is a hard game for hard men. Played with undivided interest, it is a satisfying outlet for rugged men who like physical effort. Premiums are paid for strenuous effort and for the subordination of self-interest for the good of the team. Played halfheartedly, baseball is a waste of time and energy. Baseball is not a halfway game. Players and managers who take it easy on the field come to grief and failure. To play baseball, you have to get wet all over."

—Spoken by Blue Jays manager Barney Mann, to an Englishman in Martin Quigley's novel Today's Game. *New York: Viking Press, 1965.*

"TERENCE MANN"

"The one constant through all the years, Ray, has been baseball. America has rolled by like an army of steamrollers. It has been erased like a blackboard, rebuilt and erased again. But baseball has marked the time …"

> —*The reclusive writer played by James Earl Jones in the film* Field of Dreams, *1989; written by Phil Alden Robinson.*

CHARLIE MANUEL

"There's no pressure in baseball. Pressure is when they're getting ready to cut on you for open-heart surgery and they tell you they're going to take your heart out and put it on a table. Or when they tell you they're going to put your colon in a plastic bag so they can do surgery. That's pressure. Baseball is fun."

—As Cleveland Indians manager, who has had both open-heart and intestinal surgery; quoted in Peter Schmuck's "Players' age-old problem not a big deal," Baltimore Sun, *March 3, 2002.*

WILLIE MAYS

"Baseball is a game, yes. It is also a business. But what it most truly is, is disguised combat. For all its gentility, its almost leisurely pace, baseball is violence under wraps."

—*Quoted by Arnold Hano from* A Day in the Bleachers, *1955.*

"I like to play happy. Baseball is a fun game, and I love it."

—*Quoted in* The Sporting News, *July 25, 1970.*

"SUDDEN" SAM MCDOWELL

"Baseball is both the greatest and worst thing that ever happened to me. Not because people asked too much of me, but because I asked too much of myself. As it turned out, my talent was a curse. The curse was the way I handled it and didn't handle it."

—*As a Giants pitcher. Widely attributed.*

W. O. MCGEEHAN

"Baseball is a circus, and as is the case in many a circus, the clowns and the sideshows are frequently more interesting than the big stuff in the main tent."

—*Sportswriter with the* New York Herald-Tribune.

John McGraw at the Polo Grounds, 1914.

JOHN MCGRAW

"Baseball is a National asset. Is there a boy anywhere who does not like to play? Baseball is a "play" game, but it also develops the boy's mind for it is scientific. In a physical sense, a man can be made only from a boy and a nation can be made only from its men. If Baseball assists in making better boys physically, it is directly helping to make our Nation and in doing so impresses upon all its value as a National sport."

—*The legendary New York Giants manager.*

MARY MCGRORY

"Baseball is what we were. Football is what we have become."

—From John Leo's "Now don't interrupt!" (best sayings of 1996, U.S. News & World Report, January 13, 1997).

MARSHALL MCLUHAN

"Baseball is doomed. It is the inclusive mesh of the TV image, in particular, that spells … the doom of baseball now, but it'll come back. Games go in cycle."

—*Social philosopher in 1969, quoted by Ira Berkow in* The New York Times, *February 20, 1983.*

MARIANNE MOORE

"Writing is exciting and baseball is like writing."

—*Poet and avid fan of the Brooklyn Dodgers. From "Baseball and Writing,"* The New Yorker, *December 9, 1961.*

JACK MORRIS

"Baseball has nothing to do with reality. It has nothing to do with whether children are going to bed hungry. It's just an occupation and a game. It's not going to solve world hunger or world poverty. It's not going to solve federal deficits. Baseball is a fantasy."

—What he told a reporter after a particularly disgraceful outing against the Minnesota Twins at about the same time that Ken Burns 18-hour PBS show was released. Quoted in the Toronto Star, *October 15, 1994.*

Jack Morris, 1986

RAYMOND MUNGO

"Baseball is one of the cheapest obsessions you can have."

—Confessions from Left Field: A Baseball Pilgrimage, *1983.*

"Baseball is the only game in which the Perfect Game is one in which nothing happens at all—no hits, runs, walks, errors, no men on base."

—Confessions from Left Field: A Baseball Pilgrimage, *1983.*

"… baseball is the greatest outdoor sport that has ever been known and it is thoroughly American, combining everything in the way of athletic skill, nerve, grit and honesty, and all that is best in our national character."

—Confessions from Left Field: A Baseball Pilgrimage, *1983.*

JIM MURRAY

"Baseball is not precisely a team sport. It is more a series of concerts by the artists."

—*Sportswriter,* Los Angeles Times, *1979.*

"Baseball is a game where a curve is an optical illusion, a screwball can be a pitch or a person, stealing is legal and you can spit anywhere you like except in the umpire's eye or on the ball."

—Los Angeles Times.

"The charm of baseball is that, dull as it may be on the field, it is endlessly fascinating as a rehash."

—Los Angeles Times.

RALPH NADER

"Baseball is the brainiest of games."

> —*The consumer advocate, sometimes presidential candidate and Yankees fan from "The Fan" in* The Fireside Book of Baseball, *4th edition, 1987.*

BRIAN J. NEILSON

"Baseball, more than any other sport, has lent itself to the metaphorical exploration of American life."

> —The Theatre of Sport, *1995.*

NEW YORK CLIPPER

"Base Ball is generally considered the National game amongst Americans; and right well does it deserve that appellation."

> —*December 13, 1856.*

"BASEBALL IS..."

MICHAEL NOVAK

"Baseball is as close a liturgical enactment of the white Anglo-Saxon Protestant myth as the nation has. It is a cerebral game, designed as geometrically as the city of Washington itself, born out of the Enlightenment and the philosophies so beloved of Jefferson, Madison, and Hamilton. It is to games what the *Federalist Papers* are to books: orderly, reasoned, judiciously balanced, incorporating segments of violence and collision in a larger plan of rationality, absolutely dependent on an interiorization of public rules."

—*The Catholic philosopher in* The Joy of Sports, *1976.*

"Baseball is unlike football or basketball in not being governed by a clock. Until the last out has been registered, anything can happen. Even in the last of the ninth, with two out, a team can suddenly, surprisingly, score 5 or 7 or 9 or 11 runs. It is part of the brilliant fairness of the game. You must, in the end, defeat yourself, use up in vain your own equal chances."

—*The Catholic philosopher in* The Joy of Sports, *1976.*

KEITH OLBERMANN

"Baseball is … the only sport that goes forward and backwards. You come in at the start of the game and the start of the season, or the start of your own fandom, you feel as if you were joining a river midstream."

—*Uttered at the start of* The Tenth Inning, *Ken Burns's 2010 addendum to his nine-inning 1994 documentary* Baseball.

SHARON OLDS

"Baseball is reassuring. It makes me feel as if the world is not going to blow up."

—This Sporting Life, *Milkweed Editions, 1987.*

MICHAEL OLESKER

"Baseball is a game for children played by adults who act like children."

—*In his* Baltimore Sun *column, May 21, 1998.*

WALTER O'MALLEY

"Baseball is an old-fashioned game with old-fashioned traditions."

—Los Angeles Dodgers owner Walter O'Malley's statement made in refusing to talk to the agent hired by pitching stars Sandy Koufax and Don Drysdale, who decided to use an agent in 1966 to negotiate their contracts in an effort to leverage their salaries. This summed up the owners' view.

"Baseball isn't a business, it's more like a disease."

—Widely attributed.

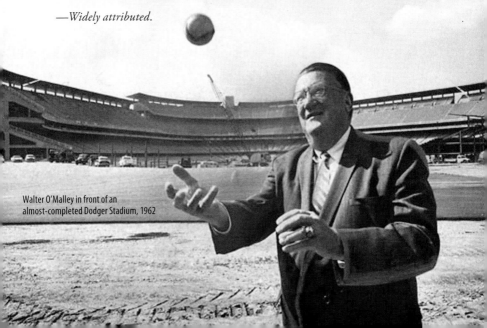

Walter O'Malley in front of an almost-completed Dodger Stadium, 1962

BUCK O'NEIL

"[Baseball] is as good as sex; it's as good as music, it fills you up."

—The late Kansas City Monarchs first baseman at the 3rd annual Negro Baseball League Reunion in Ashland, Kentucky, June 1981.

THE OXFORD ENGLISH DICTIONARY

"[Baseball is] the national field-game of the United States, a more elaborate variety of the English, rounders,—played by two sides of nine each; so called from the, bases—or bounds (usually four in number) which mark the circuit to be taken by each player of the in-side after striking the ball."

—*The* OED *notes that the first appearance of the word appears in Jane Austen's* Northanger Abbey, *written c. 1815. The sentence: "It was not very wonderful that Catherine ... should prefer cricket, base ball ... to books."*

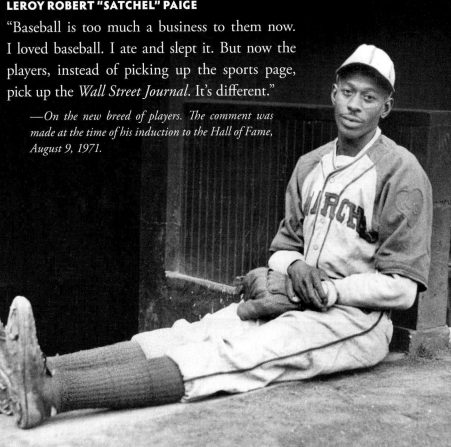

LEROY ROBERT "SATCHEL" PAIGE

"Baseball is too much a business to them now. I loved baseball. I ate and slept it. But now the players, instead of picking up the sports page, pick up the *Wall Street Journal*. It's different."

—*On the new breed of players. The comment was made at the time of his induction to the Hall of Fame, August 9, 1971.*

ROBERT B. PARKER

"Baseball is the most important thing in life that doesn't matter."

—Boston Globe, *April 15, 2005.*

GABE PAUL

"The great thing about baseball is that there's a crisis every game."

—As New York Yankees president *(1973–77)*.

CHARLES A. PEVERELLY

"[Baseball] is a game which is peculiarly suited to the American temperament and disposition; the nine innings are played in the brief space of two and one half hours, or less. From the moment the first striker takes his position, and poises his bat, it has an excitement and vim about it, until the last hand is put out in the ninth innings."

—The Book of American Pastimes, *1866.*

RICK PHALEN

"… baseball is a cold-hearted mistress."

—A Bittersweet Journey: America's Fascination with Baseball, *2000.*

"Baseball is more than a game, it is the American experience. It is competitive, tough, loud, informal, racially diverse, theatrical, spectacular, heroic, financially rewarding, and an excuse for a bunch of people to get together and raise hell."

—A Bittersweet Journey: America's Fascination with Baseball, *2000.*

JERRY PRITIKIN

"Baseball is the greatest—that's my complete and total message. It's God's gift to America, and we should treat it as such."

—"On Sports: Bleacher Preacher," Frederick C. Klein, The Wall Street Journal, *May 17, 1991. Pritikin, known as the "Bleacher Preacher," became famous during his days as a regular in the Wrigley Field bleachers during the 1980s.*

Parson Goodman: Boys! Boys! Are you not ashamed to be playing ball on the Sabbath?
Catcher: Y-Yes, sir! But they won't let us kids onter de golf links!

JOHN RAWLS

"… baseball is the only game where scoring is not done with the ball, and this has the remarkable effect of concentrating the excitement of plays at different points of the field at the same time. Will the runner cross the plate before the fielder gets to the ball and throws it to home plate, and so on."

—*The eminent philosopher (1921–2002) from a 1981 letter published in* The Boston Review, *March/April 2008.*

RICK REILLY

"Unlike almost any other game Americans play, baseball is up to its sanitary hose in human saliva."

— *"Baseball's Spitting Image,"* Sports Illustrated, *October 14, 1996.*

BOBBY RICHARDSON

"If baseball is a game of inches generally speaking, then it follows that it is specifically a game of split-seconds for second-basemen. There is no position on a baseball team which places such a high premium on timing."

—*From* Sport, *September 1965.*

PETER RICHMOND

"[Baseball] is the only game that refuses to be hurried."

—GQ, *April 1994.*

BRANCH RICKEY

"Baseball is a game of inches."

—*1957, quoted by Bob Addie in* The Washington Post.

"Baseball is good, an honorable profession, a great challenge. It has blessed me, I blessed it, and it has blessed our country."

—*Widely quoted.*

CAL RIPKEN, JR.

"Baseball is our passion, We talk about it 12 months out of the year. We care about it. We look forward to it."

—*On Maryland, quoted in* The New York Times, *February 5, 1995.*

"Baseball is like a poker game. Nobody wants to quit when he's losing; nobody wants you to quit when you're ahead."

—*Quoted in* Giants of Baseball *by Bill Gutman, 1975.*

Jackie Robinson at bat in 1947.

WILBERT ROBINSON

"Baseball is our greatest sport because it offers the unexpected thrill at any moment during a game. These thrills are often carefully planned and are only the culmination of team play. All things being equal, the team composed of nine scientific players will beat, a team of 'stars.'"

—*As manager of the Brooklyn Dodgers. Preface to* The Science of Baseball, *1922.*

WILL ROGERS

"Baseball is a skilled game. It's America's game—it, and high taxes."

—*American humorist and showman (1879–1935).*

KEN ROSENTHAL

"Baseball is a talking sport, a sport of endless debate and second-guessing."

—*"No homer, Miller sure tags all bases,"* Baltimore Sun,
October 26, 1996.

MURRAY ROSS

"Baseball is part of a civil tradition which insists that its participants be humans, while football, in the heroic mode, asks that its players be more than that."

—*"Football Red and Baseball Green,"* The Chicago Review, *1971.*

PHILLIP ROTH

"… baseball was a kind of secular church that reached into every class and region of the nation and bound us together in common concerns, loyalties, rituals, enthusiasms, and antagonisms. Baseball made me understand what patriotism was about, at its best."

— *"My Baseball Years,"* The New York Times, *April 2, 1973.*

"Baseball, with its lore and legends, its cultural power, its seasonal associations, its native authenticity, its simple rules and transparent strategies, its longeurs [sic] and thrills, its spaciousness, its suspensefulness, its peculiarly hypnotic tedium, its heroics, its nuances, its lingo, its "characters," its language, and its mythic sense of life, was the literature of my boyhood."

— *"My Baseball Years,"* The New York Times, *April 2, 1973.*

BABE RUTH

"Baseball was, is and always will be to me the best game in the world."

—*From "The Babe Ruth Story."*

"… the only real game in the world, I think, is baseball … You've got to start from way down…when you are six or seven … You've got to let it grow up with you."

—*Spoken at Babe Ruth Day at Yankee Stadium before 58,339 fans, April 27, 1947.*

NOLAN RYAN

"One of the beautiful things about baseball is that every once in a while you come into a situation where you want to, and where you have to, reach down and prove something."

—*From* Throwing Heat: The Autobiography of Nolan Ryan, *1988.*

YASUO SAKAKIBARA

"Baseball is a team game, but has wide scope for the feats of the individual player, such as an ace-pitcher or a prolific home run hitter. Closely comparable may be the *Kabuki* play, one of the traditional Japanese theaters. It is a play in which all the actors participate and yet it has a lot of famous scenes where the main actor can demonstrate his individuality and his skill. People who love *Kabuki* instinctively know what to expect in baseball. Baseball is a slow show and so is the *Kabuki*. A faster game like basketball has never gained any popularity in Japan, but baseball easily fits the tempo of life in Japan."

> —*Professor Emeritus of Economics and first chair of the Graduate School in American Studies at Doshisha University, and a past president of the Japanese Association for American Studies, quoted in Ralph Andreano,* No Joy in Mudville, *1965.*

LUKE SALISBURY

"Baseball is more like a novel than like a war. It is like an ongoing hundred-year work of art, peopled with thousands of characters, full of improbable events, anecdotes, folklore and numbers."

  —*From* The Answer is Baseball, *1989.*

WILLIAM SAROYAN

"Baseball is caring. Player and fan alike must care, or there is no game. If there's no game, there's no pennant race and no World Series. And for all any of us know there might soon be no nation at all. It is good to care—in any dimension. More Americans put their caring into baseball than into anything else I can think of—and most of them put at least a little of it there. Baseball can be trusted, as great art can, and bad art can't."

—*Quoted from* Sports Illustrated *and used in a mass mailing to* Sports Illustrated *advertisers, June 8, 1959.*

"ANNIE SAVOY"

"[Baseball] is never boring. Which makes it like sex."

—Her soliloquy at the beginning of the movie Bull Durham *(1988). Savoy is played by Susan Sarandon. The script was written by Ron Shelton.*

RICHARD SCHICKEL

"In myth, baseball is a circle of light in a world increasingly darkened by corruption. It is a clean, green place that absorbs, preserves and reflects back upon us, through the heroically magnified deeds of its adepts, the purity with which, as children open to and eager for enchantment, we first encountered it. This game is a mind game, an ideal, and one that seems an almost lost legend for which people nowadays mourn, as they do for many things that graced a more leisurely and miraculous time. But baseball is also a reality, a game played by ungrammatical men who, like most people, have grown up without necessarily growing wise. They chew tobacco, indulge in alcoholic beverages and do not always fend off the groupies with the fervor expected of moral exemplars."

—Time *movie critic in his review of* The Natural, *May 14, 1984.*

GEORGE BERNARD SHAW

"Baseball is swift, intense, and (as to what it is all about) inscrutable."

—From his 1924 essay "An American Baseball Game," reprinted in
A Freshman Miscellany, *edited by Karl J. Holzknecht, 1930.*

WILFRID SHEED

"...Baseball is not a set of isolated explosions like football, but a steady, timeless pleasure that builds as gracefully as it plays—and can only have one climax.

'Do not mess with it, gentlemen.'"

—*From "Sliding for Dollars: The Split Season of 1981," in* Baseball and Lesser Sports, *by HarperCollins, New York, 1991. Sheed is lamenting the playoffs.*

MARK SHIELDS

"Baseball is about personal and individual accountability. It is relentlessly democratic."

—*Syndicated columnist.*

BRADD SHORE

"Many argued that baseball is only a game whose importance paled in the face of death and destruction left behind by the earthquake. But when the series resumed, the restoration of baseball—game and ritual—was for many like awakening from a bad dream to look again upon the real world."

—Emory University anthropologist commenting on the 1989 World Series, which was interrupted by an earthquake. Quoted in Emory Family, *Spring 1996.*

WRIGLEY FIELD

CHUCK SHRIVER

"The beauty and joy of baseball is not having to explain it."

> —*As Chicago Cubs public relations man, widely quoted.*

RED SMITH

"Baseball is dull only to dull minds. Today's game is always different from yesterday's game."

> —*Columnist in* The New York Herald Tribune, *quoted in* The Red Smith Reader, *1983.*

ALBERT GOODWILL SPALDING

"Base ball gives … a growing boy self-poise and self-reliance. Base ball is a man maker."

—*Quoted by David Quentin Voigt in* America Through Baseball, *1976.*

"[Base ball] is the exponent of American Courage, Confidence, Combativeness; American Dash, Discipline, Determination; American Energy, Eagerness, Enthusiasm; American Pluck, Persistency, Performance; American Spirit, Sagacity, Success; American Vim, Vigor, Virility.

Base ball is the American Game *par excellence*, because its playing demands Brain and Brawn, and American manhood supplies these ingredients in quantity sufficient to spread over the entire continent …

Base ball is a democratic game."

—America's National Game, *1911.*

"SPENSER"

"Baseball is worth watching, whoever plays it."

> —*Robert B. Parker, as spoken by his prime detective who appears in the Spenser novels and the "Spenser for Hire" television series. Quoted from* USA Baseball Weekly, *May 17, 1991.*

J. G. TAYLOR SPINK

"Baseball is the American success story ... It is, moreover, a great common ground on which bartenders and bishops, clergymen and bosses, bankers and laborers meet with true equality and understanding. The game has proved in everyday language that democracy works."

> —*As editor of* The Sporting News.

OUR BASEBALL HEROES.

206

SPIRIT OF THE TIMES

Of all out-door sports, base-ball is that in which the greatest number of our people participate either as players or as spectators. ... It is a pastime that best suits the temperament of our people. The accessories being less costly than those of the turf, the acquatic course, or the cricket-field, it is an economic game, and within the easy reach of the masses.

—*An 1867 issue of this sporting newspaper.*

SAUL STEINBERG

"Baseball is an allegorical play about America, a poetic, complex, and subtle play of courage, fear, good luck, mistakes, patience about fate, and sober self-esteem ... It is impossible to understand America without a thorough knowledge of baseball."

—*The artist known for, among other things, his* New Yorker *covers. Quoted by Harold Rosenberg, in* Saul Steinberg, *1978.*

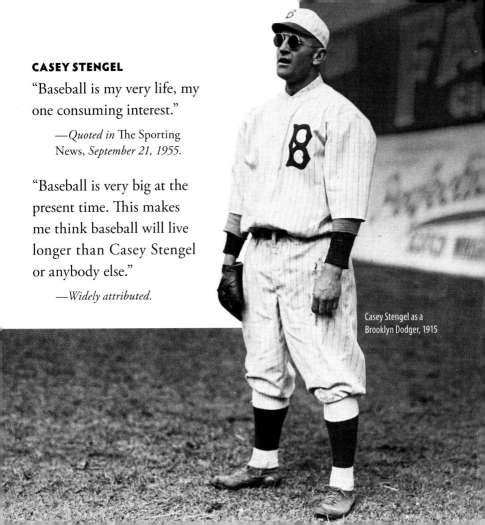

CASEY STENGEL

"Baseball is my very life, my one consuming interest."

—*Quoted in* The Sporting News, *September 21, 1955.*

"Baseball is very big at the present time. This makes me think baseball will live longer than Casey Stengel or anybody else."

—*Widely attributed.*

Casey Stengel as a Brooklyn Dodger, 1915

ICHIRO SUZUKI

"Baseball is just baseball."

—When asked if he would have trouble making adjustments to the American major leagues, Seattle Post-Intelligencer, *March 30, 2001.*

Ichiro at Shea Stadium, June 25, 2008.

President Taft at Senators vs. White Sox game, Aug. 13, 1912

WILLIAM HOWARD TAFT

"The game of baseball is a clean straight game, and it summons to its presence everybody who enjoys clean, straight athletics. It furnishes amusement to the thousands and thousands. And I like it for two reasons—first, because I enjoy it myself and second, because if by the presence of the temporary chief magistrate such a healthy amusement can be encouraged, I want to encourage it."

—Published in The Sporting News, *May 4, 1910, from a speech given in St. Louis. This is how Taft's role as First Fan was described in the 1911* Spalding's Official Base Ball Guide: *"President Taft believes in Base Ball. ... He tells his friends that it is a pastime worth every man's while and advises them to banish the blues by going to a ball game and waking up with the enthusiasts of the bleachers who permit no man to be grouchy among them."*

DANIEL J. TAYLOR

"Baseball is a game with the power to restore faith. In its infancy baseball healed the wounds of the Civil War. The Black Sox scandal of 1919 ushered in the '20s and the great Yankee teams featuring America's most famous orphan. Blacks could eventually play major league baseball even though they couldn't sit in the front of the bus. Resurrection is a fact of baseball, just as it is of religion."

—*The sports historian, Lawrence University, from his essay "Baseball: More Than Just America's Game."*

"… baseball is downright lazy. It features anticipation as much as action. The game's lack of continuity is exasperating to the uninitiated, but to true believers it affords a wealth of beloved intervals, during back to double-play depth, the third baseman edging in for the hunt, the batter choking up. Yes, baseball is paradoxical, but so is American culture."

—*From his essay "Baseball: More Than Just America's Game."*

JOHN THORN

"Baseball is the writer's game. From the Elysian Fields of Hoboken to the green fields of the mind, the grand old game and the printed word were made for each other."

—*From the Introduction to* The Armchair Book of Baseball, *1985.*

1865 baseball game at Elysian Fields, Hoboken, N.J.

JOE TORRE

"Baseball is the only thing I ever wanted to do. When I was 16 years old, my brother Frank said, 'You'd better become a catcher, because you're too big and fat to do anything else.' Well, I took his advice. It was a quick way to get to the big leagues, and I've never regretted it."

—*As newly installed manager of the Los Angeles Dodgers. Quoted in* Time, *March 27, 2008.*

MANNY TRILLO

"The best thing about baseball is that you can do something about yesterday tomorrow."

—*As a Philadelphia Phillies infielder; widely quoted.*

TED TURNER

"Baseball is a game, a big game, but only a game. Collecting garbage is more important. What would you rather have, a yard filled with garbage or a ticket to a ball game?"

—*1978.*

MARK TWAIN

"Baseball is the very symbol, the outward and visible expression of the drive and push and rush and struggle of the raging, tearing, booming nineteenth century."

—April 8, 1889, at a banquet at Delmonico's restaurant, New York, honoring baseball players returning from the 1888–1889 Spalding round-the-world tour.

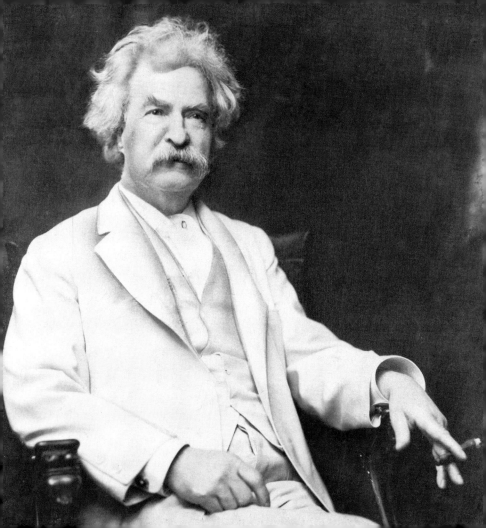

PETER V. UEBERROTH

"Baseball is a realm of fairness and order where imagery, mysticism, and alchemy in the confines of the baseball diamond tickle the little boy or girl in all of us. Though it appears to be detached from the real world in many respects, it often reflects the best and worst of our society."

> —*The Former Baseball Commissioner from the Foreword to* The Armchair Book of Baseball, *1985.*

"Baseball is a public trust. Players turn over, owners turn over and certain commissioners turn over. But baseball goes on."

> —The New York Times, *May 12, 1985.*

JOHN UPDIKE

"Baseball is a game of the long season, of relentless and gradual averaging-out."

—*"Hub Fans Bid Kid Adieu,"* The New Yorker, *October 22, 1960.*

"... baseball, with its graceful intermittences of action, its immense and tranquil field sparsely settled with poised men in white, its dispassionate mathematics, seems to me best suited to accommodate, and to be ornamented by, a loner. It is an essentially lonely game."

—*"Hub Fans Bid Kid Adieu,"* The New Yorker, *October 22, 1960.*

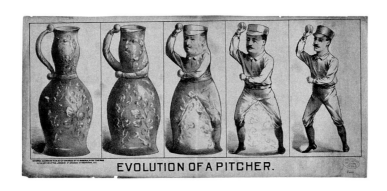

EVOLUTION OF A PITCHER.

GEORGE VECSEY

"Baseball is a wonderful game for hero-worshipping, for ritual, for imitation. It used to be that all you needed was a pink rubber ball and a wall, and you could be Sal (the Barber) Maglie and Willie Mays with the basket catch and Gil Hodges with the long stretch at first and Roy Campanella circling under a popup, for hours on end."

—The New York Times, *August 14, 1994.*

"Even though its leaders defy nature by putting in artificial turf and domed stadiums, and the pay can only be called unbelievable, baseball is the only sport in harmony with nature. It is real life. Everything else is the off-season."

—The New York Times, *March 15, 1992.*

"The nice thing about baseball is that it shares its grace with the uninitiated. Just the sound of a baseball game from a passing car radio makes a person relax, like the first warm breeze of the season."

—The New York Times, *March 15, 1992.*

BILL VEECK

"Baseball is almost the only orderly thing in a very unorderly world. If you get three strikes, even Edward Bennett Williams can't get you off."

—Sports Illustrated, *June 2, 1975.*

"Baseball is like our society. It's becoming homogenized, computerized. People identify with the swashbuckling individuals, not polite little men who field their position well. Sir Galahad had a big following— but I'll bet Lancelot had more."

—*Quoted in a* Washington Post *interview, February 11, 1971.*

"Baseball is the only game left for people. To play basketball now, you have to be 7 ft. 6 in. To play football, you have to be the same width."

—*Widely quoted.*

"Baseball is the only thing besides the paper clip that hasn't changed."

—*1974.*

TOM VERDUCCI

"Baseball is as egalitarian as we like to think our country is. Down to your last chance, you can't call time-out and design a play for John Elway or Michael Jordan. The baseball gods typically hand such moments to someone who looks like the kid who bags your groceries, someone like 170-pound Craig Counsell. Who can't root for that?"

—Sports Illustrated, *April 6, 1998.*

GENE VIDAL

"Baseball is the favorite American sport because it's so slow. Any idiot can follow it. And just about any idiot can play it."

—*Aviation pioneer and father of Gore Vidal; quoted in* The New York Review of Books, *October 18, 1973. Reprinted in Vidal, Gore,* Matters of Fact and of Fiction; Essays 1973-1976. *New York: Random House, 1977.*

EARL WEAVER

"Baseball is pitching, 3-run homers, and fundamentals."

—*Quoted by Tom Boswell in* How Life Imitates the World Series, *1982.*

"You can't sit on a lead and run a few plays into the line and just kill the clock. You've got to throw the ball over the goddamn plate and give the other man his chance. That's why baseball is the greatest game of them all."

—*Baltimore Orioles manager, quoted in Roger Angell,* The Summer Game, *1972.*

WES WESTRUM

"Baseball is like church. Many attend but few understand."

—*San Francisco Giants coach, 1962.*

WALT WHITMAN

"Baseball is our game—the American game. It will take our people out of doors, fill them with oxygen, give them a larger physical stoicism. Tend to relieve us from being a nervous, dyspeptic set. Repair these losses, and be a blessing to us."

—*Widely attributed.*

Walt Whitman, 1862

TOM WICKER

"Baseball is to me the remembered taste of an ice-cold bellywasher sneaked between innings, against all rules."

—*Good Old Country Hardball*, Esquire, *June 1983.*

MICHAEL WILBON

"Baseball, unlike the NFL and NBA, is still largely a regional game. Greg Maddux may be going to the Hall of Fame but he's not beloved everywhere, by everybody."

—Washington Post, *June 20, 2001.*

TIM WILES

"And then there is my wife. Just as I was about to launch into a speech about how *Bull Durham* 'isn't really about baseball,' she preempted me by saying 'I don't even think *baseball* is really about baseball.'"

—*Director of Research at the National Baseball Hall of Fame, 2010 with a major assist from Marie Wiles.*

GEORGE F. WILL

"It is said that baseball is only a game. Yes, and the Grand Canyon is only a hole in Arizona."

—From *"A Baseball Game is Not an Iowa Caucus,"* The Washington Post, *October 13, 1983.*

Polo Grounds, New York, Oct. 13, 1910

TED WILLIAMS

"Baseball is the only field of endeavor where a man can succeed three times out of ten and be considered a good performer."

—Hall of Fame outfielder, 1967.

"In my opinion, baseball is the hardest sport to play. To narrow it down further, hitting a baseball is the single most difficult thing there is in sports. It takes more skill to hit a baseball than it does to do anything else."

—Widely quoted.

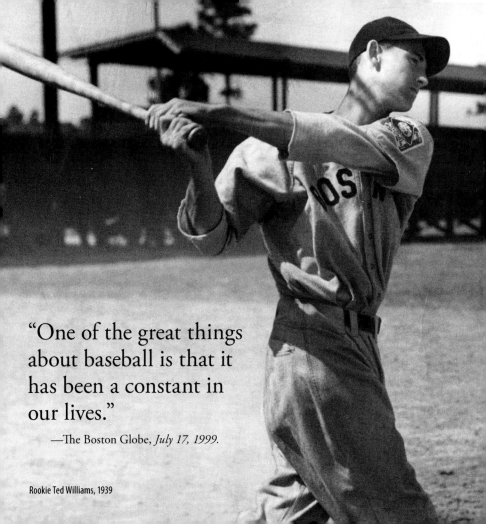

"One of the great things about baseball is that it has been a constant in our lives."

—The Boston Globe, *July 17, 1999.*

Rookie Ted Williams, 1939

EARL WILSON

"A baseball game is simply a nervous breakdown divided into nine innings."

—*The syndicated columnist.*

PHILIP WRIGLEY

"Baseball is too much of a sport to be a business and too much of a business to be a sport."

—*Chicago Cubs owner,* Forbes, *April 12, 1982.*

"ZELIG"

"I love baseball, you know it doesn't have to mean anything, it's just very beautiful to watch."

—*Woody Allen, from the movie of the same name, Orion Pictures (1983).*

ACKNOWLEDGMENTS

First and foremost, Skip McAfee for access to his world-class collection of baseball quotations and his direct editorial help with this compilation including fact-checking and index construction. Also thanks to: Frank Ceresi, Peter Golenbock, Joe Goulden, Mark McGuire, Bob Skole, Tim Wiles, Tim Wendell, and Martin Zelnik.

The author can be reached through his website, www.pauldicksonbooks.com, or at P.O. Box 280, Garrett Park, MD 20896.

IMAGE SOURCE REFERENCE

INDEX

"BASEBALL IS…

"BASEBALL IS..."